Barack Obama often played pick-up basketball games to escape the tensions of the presidential race. He is dressed for a workout with the University of North Carolina's Tar Heels in Chapel Hill (April 2008).

President Barack Obama

PLATE 1

Doll, right. Appearing on *The Tonight Show* with Jay Leno, Michelle Obama wore a J. Crew "Italian Deco" tank top of silk twill over a sheath skirt in a shadow check (October 27, 2008). *Left.* The matching cardigan is fastened at the neckline by a multi-color "vintage" stone brooch.

*First Lady
Michelle Obama*

PLATE 2

M

S

Sasha Obama

Malia Obama

Left. Sasha Obama (b. 2001) wore an "A"-cut dress featuring a fabric corsage at the 2008 Democratic Convention in Denver, Colorado. *Right.* At the Convention, Malia Obama (b. 1998) wore a dress featuring a bathing-suit top with a bow and softly pleated skirt. Both girls wore shoulder-length curls.

PLATE 3

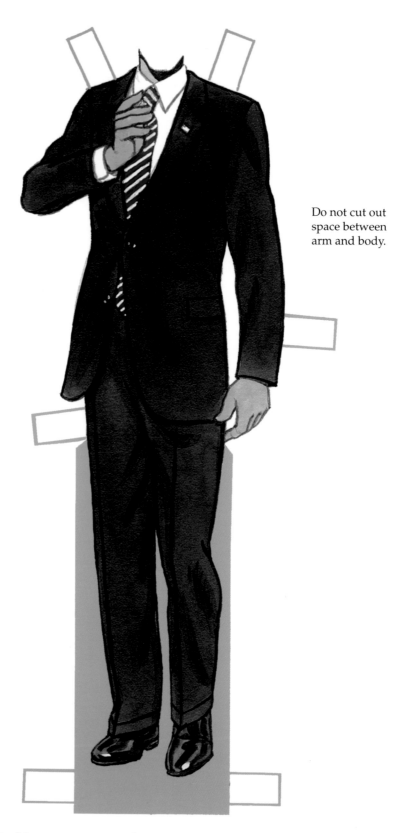

Do not cut out space between arm and body.

For his acceptance speech on August 28, 2008, at the Democratic Convention, Mr. Obama wore a wool single-breasted suit by Hart Schaffner Marx, a silk tie, and an American flag lapel pin.

PLATE 4

Do not cut out
space between
arm and body.

Michelle Obama wore a dress by designer Thakoon Panichgul at the
Convention for the acceptance speech. Outstanding for both its cut and
the flamboyant black-on-red print fabric, the dress had a squared scoop
neckline, accented with three silver brooches by Erickson Beamon.

PLATE 5

Sasha, *left*, wore a formal bubble-skirted dress with a vertical stripe for her father's acceptance speech at the Convention. Malia, *right*, wore a formal dress of lace over silk, featuring a wide satin waist sash and matching straps.

PLATE 6

Do not cut out
space between
arm and body.

On Election Night, November 4, 2008, for his acceptance speech,
President-Elect Obama wore a custom-made, two-button worsted wool
Hart Schaffner Marx suit.

PLATE 7

For her husband's Election Night acceptance speech, Michelle Obama wore a Narciso Rodriguez satin dress with a cardigan. The dress's waist had crisscross panels. She wore diamond bangle bracelets and oversized looped diamond earrings by Loree Rodkin.

PLATE 8

For their father's presidential acceptance speech, Sasha, *left*, wore an "Iris and Ivy" dress by Gerson & Gerson. It had a bolero jacket with three-quarter-length sleeves and a large neckline bow. The full skirt had an overlay of sheer, patterned with floral bouquets. *Right*. Malia's silk taffeta Biscotti, Inc., party dress featured a bubble hem and matching jacket.

PLATE 9

Do not cut out space between arm and body.

On November 10, 2008, President Bush and Mrs. Bush gave the Obamas a tour of their new home, the White House. The President-Elect wore a single-breasted, two-button worsted suit, a patterned silk tie, and an American flag lapel pin.

PLATE 10

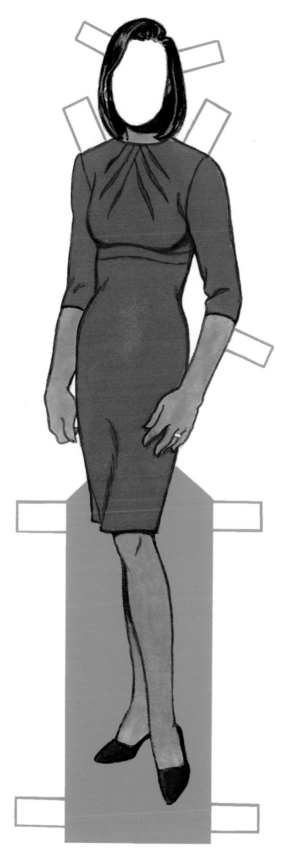

For the White House tour, the First Lady-Elect chose a Maria Pinto sheath dress with three-quarter-length sleeves, a hint of an Empire waistline, and stitched-down diagonal pleats falling from the jewel-collar neckline.

PLATE 11

Do not cut out
space between
arm and body.

For the swearing-in, on January 20, 2009, Mr. Obama wore a single-breasted suit with a checked silk tie and an American flag lapel pin. His overcoat was a single-breasted cashmere blend. Both garments were from Hart Schaffner Marx.

PLATE 12

On Inauguration Day, Michelle Obama chose a custom-made Isabel Toledo dress and topcoat of Swiss wool lace over wool with Jimmy Choo shoes. *Left.* The sheath had a matching cardigan. At the neckline, she wore an imitation-diamond Victorian brooch by Carole Tanenbaum. Her earrings were pavé diamond studs. *Right.* The First Lady, in the topcoat and J. Crew gloves, holds the Lincoln Bible.

PLATE 13

On Inauguration Day, Sasha and Malia wore outfits from Crewcuts by J. Crew. *Left.* Sasha wore a three-quarter-length wool coat. Her skirt, gloves, and broad muffler matched the satin bow-tied ribbon coat belt. *Right.* Malia chose a double-breasted wool coat, belted with a satin ribbon.

PLATE 14

Do not cut out space between arm and body.

For his Inaugural Ball outfit, President Obama wore a custom-made, all-wool tuxedo from Hart Schaffner Marx, featuring a one-button, satin-notch lapelled jacket and single-pleat trousers. On his lapel he wore his American flag pin.

PLATE 15

The First Lady's silk chiffon Inaugural Ball gown, designed by Jason Wu, was lined with crepe and embellished with organza flowers and Swarovski crystals. Mrs. Obama wore jewelry by Loree Rodkin: diamond drop earrings, bangle bracelets, and an outsized diamond signet ring.

PLATE 16